# FOX

### by CAROLINE ARNOLD
### photographs by RICHARD HEWETT
### MORROW JUNIOR BOOKS • *New York*

PHOTO CREDITS: Permission to use the following photographs is gratefully acknowledged: the Baltimore Zoo, p. 17; Terry Lincoln, the Dakota Zoo, p. 19; Caroline Arnold, p. 27; Arthur Arnold, p. 32.

The text type is 14-point Palatino.

Library of Congress Cataloging-in-Publication Data    Arnold, Caroline.    Fox/by Caroline Arnold; photographs by Richard Hewett.    p. cm. Includes index.    Summary: Describes these members of the dog family that are easily recognized by their long snouts, large ears, and bushy tails and that live in many different habitats.    ISBN 0-688-13728-8 (trade)—ISBN 0-688-13729-6 (library)    1. Foxes—North America—Juvenile literature.    [1. Foxes.]    I. Hewett, Richard, ill.    II. Title.    QL737.C22A75 1996    599.74'442—dc20    95-35229    CIP AC

## ACKNOWLEDGMENTS

We are grateful to the staffs and volunteers at the following zoos for their cheerful assistance while we were working on this project: the Los Angeles Zoo, the California Living Museum (Bakersfield), the Living Desert Wildlife and Botanical Park (Palm Desert), all in California; the Baltimore Zoo, Maryland; and the Dakota Zoo, Bismarck, North Dakota. We also appreciate the help of our friends Don Jim and Barney Schlinger. And, as always, we thank our editor, Andrea Curley, for her continued support.

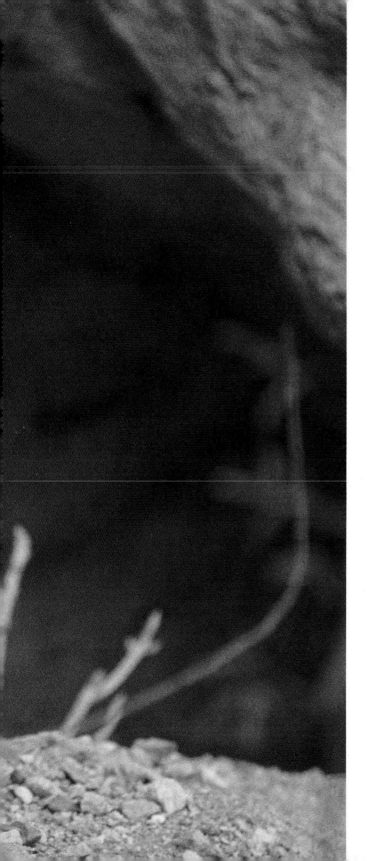

## THE KIT FOX

As the afternoon sun sinks in the sky, a kit fox rests on a rocky ledge and looks out on the surrounding desert landscape. Its eyes and ears are alert as it watches for the movements of small animals in the shadows and listens for noises. Soon the air will cool, and it will be time for the fox to go hunting. With sharp senses and quick reflexes, the tiny kit fox is an expert at catching the leaping rodents, scurrying lizards, and unwary birds that are its food. This wily and resourceful predator is the smallest North American fox. It shares many characteristics with other kinds of foxes, but it is unique in its ability to thrive in the dry and often extreme conditions of the desert.

## AT HOME IN THE DESERT

The kit fox is found in desert and semidesert regions of the western United States and in northwestern and north-central Mexico. Every part of the kit fox's body helps it to survive in these arid regions. In summer, daytime temperatures in the desert soar to more than 100° F (37.7° C), but in winter and at night, the desert air can be freezing cold. Thick fur protects the kit fox's body from both heat and cold. Stiff tufts of hair on the soles of its feet protect them from the hot ground. They also help the feet get a better grip when the fox is walking or running across loose sandy surfaces.

The inner surfaces of the kit fox's ears are covered with thick fur that helps to keep out sand. As with many other mammals that live in the desert, the kit fox has ears that are unusually large, and this helps it stay cool. The large surface of the ears provides space for many tiny blood vessels, and as desert breezes blow across them, the blood inside the ears is cooled. The blood then flows to the rest of the fox's body and cools it.

Kit foxes also cool off by opening their mouths and panting. As water evaporates from the tongue, it takes heat away from the body. (Foxes do not have sweat glands except for a few between their toes.)

The kit fox's light-colored coat helps keep its body cool by reflecting the sun's heat. It also makes the fox hard to see against the sandy color of the desert floor. This helps the fox both to hide from danger and to sneak up on the animals that are its food.

Desert-dwelling foxes are often not as big as other foxes. The kit fox weighs only 6 pounds (2.7 kilograms) or less; in fact, it gets its name because its small size makes it resemble a young fox, called a *kit* or a *pup*. The fennec fox of the Sahara Desert in Africa weighs only 4 pounds (1.8 kilograms) and is the smallest fox in the world. Because their bodies are smaller, these foxes need less food; and in a desert environment, where food is scarce, that advantage can increase their chances for survival.

Kit fox (below) and fennec fox (above).

*Kit fox in its zoo enclosure.*

## WATCHING FOXES

There are twenty-one species of foxes in the world. With their long snouts, large ears, and bushy tails, they are easy to recognize. Foxes live in many different kinds of habitats, ranging from deserts to arctic tundra and from dense woodlands to open plains. The species that live in North America are the red fox, gray fox, island gray fox, arctic fox, kit fox, and swift fox.

You may have foxes close to where you live. You can also learn about them by visiting a zoo or wildlife park. Many zoos that feature desert wildlife have exhibits of kit foxes.

When foxes are kept in enclosures resembling their natural habitat, they behave much as they do in the wild. Zoos also play an important role in breeding endangered species of foxes and in caring for animals that have been injured and can no longer live on their own in the wild.

11

## FOXES OF NORTH AMERICA

The **red fox** is the most widespread of all fox species and is found throughout most of the Northern Hemisphere, ranging northward to the Arctic Circle in North America, Europe, and Asia and southward as far as Central America and the deserts of North Africa. European settlers brought red foxes to Australia in the mid-1800s, and they now live there in the wild as well. Red foxes are found in a wide variety of habitats, including woodlands, mountains, deserts, and farmland. Some even live in cities, where they eat rodents, garbage, and whatever else they can find.

When most people think of foxes, they picture the red fox, with its large white-tipped tail and brilliant flame-colored fur. Actually, the color of red fox fur varies from gray to red but is usually a reddish brown, which makes the fox easy to spot against green grass or on white snow during winter.

The red fox is the largest of the North American foxes, weighing from 6 ½ to 24 pounds (2.9 to 10.9 kilograms). The head-and-body length of red foxes ranges from 23 to 35 inches (58.9 to 89.7 centimeters), and the tail is between 13 and 19 inches (33.3 and 48.7 centimeters) long. As with other foxes, males and females look alike, but females are usually somewhat smaller.

**Gray foxes** are medium-sized foxes with coarse, mostly gray coats and black-tipped tails. Parts of the head, neck, and legs are a rusty color, and there is a dark stripe down the center of the back. Gray foxes are about as heavy as red foxes, but because their legs are shorter, they appear to be smaller. The weight of gray foxes ranges from 5½ to 15½ pounds (2.5 to 7 kilograms) and their head-and-body length can be from 19 to 28½ inches (48.7 to 73.1 centimeters). The tail is between 10½ and 17½ inches (26.9 and 44.9 centimeters) long.

The gray fox lives in North and South America and is found as far north as the United States border with Canada and as far south as Venezuela and Colombia. It is relatively common in the United States and can be seen everywhere except in the northern Rockies, parts of the Great Basin Desert, and the state of Washington. The gray fox lives in a wide variety of habitats and is often found close to farms and cities.

The **island gray fox** is very similar in appearance to the gray fox except that it has a slightly shorter tail. Both species have the unusual ability to climb tall trees, where they hunt birds, squirrels, and other tree-dwelling animals. The island gray fox lives only in the Channel Islands off the coast of southern California.

Arctic foxes are short, compact, densely furred animals that thrive in some of the coldest places on earth. They live in arctic regions throughout much of the Northern Hemisphere and can survive at temperatures as low as -76° F (-60° C). Unlike other foxes, arctic foxes even have thick fur on the soles of their feet, which helps keep them warm as they walk across snow and ice.

Arctic foxes range greatly in size, weighing from 3 to nearly 20 pounds (1.4 to 9.1 kilograms). The average head-and-body length for males is 21½ inches (55.1 centimeters) and for females, 21 inches (53.8 centimeters). Compared to other foxes, arctic foxes have smaller ears, shorter muzzles, and shorter legs. Their tails range in length from 10 to 13½ inches (25.6 to 34.6 centimeters). When sleeping, an arctic fox curls up tight, like a ball,
using its tail as a thick furry blanket.

A fox's fur consists of a short dense coat that grows next to the skin and an outer layer of longer, coarse guard hairs. With arctic foxes the underfur is especially thick. As with other foxes, the arctic fox sheds its winter coat in spring and grows it back in fall.

The fur of arctic foxes can be either blue or white—and these colors change with the season. White foxes are pure white in winter and gray or brown in summer. Blue foxes are not actually blue but have coats that range from pearl gray to black in summer and turn somewhat lighter in winter. White foxes tend to live in interior regions, such as Alaska and Siberia, where there is a lot of snow in winter. Their white fur makes them hard to see against the snow. Blue foxes are found more often in coastal areas along the Arctic Ocean.

*Arctic fox.*

Arctic fox fur is the warmest kind of mammal fur there is. It is highly prized by humans, who use it to make hats, coats, and other clothing. Every year, about 100,000 wild arctic foxes are trapped and killed for their pelts. Arctic foxes are also raised on "fur farms." Most fox fur used commercially comes from farmed animals. Although the use of animal skins for clothing has declined in recent years, fox farming and the trapping of foxes for their fur are still important industries in many parts of the world.

The **kit fox** is a small slender fox about the size of a domestic cat. It is found in Texas, New Mexico, Arizona, Utah, south-central California, Nevada, Idaho, Oregon, and parts of northern Mexico. The color of the kit fox's coat varies but is usually gray along the back; buff or orange on the shoulders, legs, and chest; and white underneath. Kit foxes weigh between 3 and 6 pounds (1.4 and 2.7 kilograms) and have a head-and-body length between 14 and 20 inches (35.9 and 51.3 centimeters). The tail is between 9 and 12½ inches (23.1 and 32.1 centimeters) long.

The **swift fox** is found on prairies in eastern Montana, North and South Dakota, Wyoming, Colorado, Nebraska, Kansas, Oklahoma, northwestern Texas, and parts of Alberta and Saskatchewan in Canada. The swift fox and the kit fox have many similarities, including light-colored coats, large ears, nocturnal habits, and the ability to sprint at great speeds over short distances. The swift fox is slightly larger than the kit fox and, for its size, has smaller ears, a broader snout, and a shorter tail than the kit fox. Swift foxes weigh between 4 and 6 pounds (1.8 and 2.7 kilograms). Head-and-body length is between 15 and 22 inches (38.5 and 56.4 centimeters), and the tail is between 9 and 11 inches (23.1 and 28.2 centimeters) long.

In places where both kit foxes and swift foxes live, they sometimes interbreed. Usually, animals can breed with one another only if they are from the same species or if they are closely related. Some scientists classify kit foxes and swift foxes as members of the same species and consider the kit fox a subspecies of the swift fox. (When groups of animals within a species differ slightly from one another, scientists classify each group as a subspecies.) Other scientists disagree and think that there are enough differences between the two types of foxes to classify them as separate species. In any case, the two foxes can be distinguished from each other by their different sizes and habitats.

*Kit fox (above); swift fox (below).*

## FOXES AT RISK

In the early 1800s, swift foxes were common on the Great Plains of the United States and Canada, but they gradually disappeared as people from the eastern part of the continent moved west and converted the prairies to farmland. Swift foxes suffered both from loss of habitat and from eating poisoned bait put out by farmers to kill wolves and coyotes. Swift foxes were also hunted for their fur.

By the mid-1900s, there were few swift foxes left in the United States, and in Canada they had become extinct. Since then, new methods of pest control and laws protecting swift foxes have helped their numbers grow in the United States. Beginning in 1983, swift foxes born in the U.S. were released in parts of Canada, with the hope that they would become reestablished there.

The kit fox thrives in most of the places where it lives, but one subspecies, the San Joaquin kit fox, in California, is endangered. Every year hundreds of San Joaquin kit foxes die because of the loss of their habitat, cave-ins of their burrows caused by off-road vehicles, poisoning, and illegal shooting and trapping. These foxes were once abundant in much of the Central Valley of California. Today, only about 5,000 San Joaquin kit foxes remain, and most of them live on the Carrizo Plain, a 400-square-mile (1,036-square-kilometer) grassland that they share with elk, pronghorn antelope, and other native wildlife. Although kit foxes are protected in California, they continue to be at risk.

Island gray foxes live only on six small islands off the coast of southern California, and their numbers have never been great. They are considered a threatened species in California and are protected from hunters.

Red foxes, gray foxes, and arctic foxes are not endangered. In fact, red foxes have adapted so well to life near people that their numbers are steadily increasing.

## THE DOG FAMILY

Foxes are part of the dog family, or canids, a group that includes approximately thirty-five species worldwide. Some other canids are wolves, coyotes, jackals, wild dogs, dingoes, and domestic dogs. Scientists believe that domestic dogs are descended from wolves that were tamed by people about 12,000 years ago.

Wild canids that live in North America are foxes, wolves, and coyotes. Of these, wolves are the largest and can weigh as much as 176 pounds (80 kilograms). Coyotes are medium-sized and weigh up to 35 pounds (15.9 kilograms). They can live in a wide variety of habitats and are highly adaptable. Coyotes are the most widespread of all wild canids in North America and can be found almost everywhere.

Although each canid species has

*Coyote (left); wolf (right).*

*A kit fox grooms itself.*

its own unique characteristics, they all have many features and behaviors in common. Most canids have long legs that are well suited for long-distance running. Each foot is padded with tough leathery skin and has a long nail at the end of each toe. The hard nails help the feet to grip the ground when running and to loosen dirt when digging. Canids also use their nails to scratch themselves and to groom and clean their fur.

Most canids, including foxes, have five toes on each of their front feet and four toes on each back foot. The fifth small toe on each front foot is called the *dewclaw*. It is located above the foot, on the inside of each foreleg. The dewclaw helps the animal pull down prey and hold it with its foot.

Canids have strong jaws and sharp teeth that are well suited to catching, killing, and eating other animals. Canids are meat eaters, or carnivores. Although most of them eat meat as their main food, their diets may also include insects, eggs, fruits, and berries.

Foxes have typical canid teeth, and in most fox species the total number of teeth is forty-two. The six pairs of small incisor teeth in the front of the mouth are used to nip and hold objects. Behind the incisors are four sharp canine teeth, one on each side of the upper and lower jaws. The large pointed canines are characteristic of all meat-eating mammals and are used both to kill and to tear apart prey. Behind the canine teeth are sixteen premolars and ten molars. The last premolar in the upper jaw and the first molar in the lower jaw are called *carnassials*. These large pointed teeth cut against each other like the blades of scissors and are good for ripping and tearing. The flat molars in the back of the mouth are used for grinding and chewing.

Foxes have longer, narrower snouts than most other canids. Their thin snouts allow them to poke between rocks and under bushes in search of food. On the snout, there are sensitive hairs, called *vibrissae*, that help the fox to feel objects.

*A kit fox digs with strong paws.*

Foxes have excellent hearing and can detect sounds well above the range that humans can hear. These high-pitched sounds, called *ultrasounds,* are made by many of the rodents that are the foxes' prey. When a kit fox hears the noises made by a rodent moving around in a shallow tunnel underneath the ground, the fox digs up the dirt with its paws, opens the tunnel, and catches the animal.

The kit fox's main prey is the kangaroo rat. This small rodent thrives in the dry places where the kit fox lives. Kit foxes also eat rabbits, mice, insects, birds, lizards, and occasionally the juicy fruits of cactus plants. Kit foxes get enough moisture in their food so that they can manage without drinking water if it is not available. They drink regularly in captivity and whenever they can find water in the wild.

*Dove (above left); desert kangaroo rat (above right); long-nosed leopard lizard (below)—all sometimes food for kit foxes.*

*A kit fox uses its bushy tail for balance.*

A fox's thick furry tail is sometimes called a *brush*. It helps the fox be a good hunter. The tail is used for balance and to guide the fox, the way a rudder on a boat is used for steering. With the help of its tail, the fox can maneuver sharply and change direction in a hurry.

All foxes have extremely quick reflexes and can run fast and turn quickly. A kit fox must be extremely agile to catch fast-moving animals like kangaroo rats. These tiny rodents can jump several feet in a single bound. Kit foxes are surefooted and sometimes even climb small trees in search of prey.

## THE BURROW

Most foxes live in dens at least part of the year. Some species, such as the gray fox, prefer to make their dens in rock crevices or in hollow trees, but most foxes live in burrows underground. Kit foxes and swift foxes use their burrows year-round. The burrow helps the fox stay warm in winter and cool in the midday sun of summer.

Kit fox burrows are usually located in open areas, often where the ground rises slightly. This helps keep out water from heavy rains or melting snow.

Kit foxes often just enlarge and then use the abandoned burrows of badgers, rabbits, or other animals rather than dig their own. Burrow sizes vary; there are small dens used by a single animal and much larger ones inhabited by one or more females and their pups. A kit fox may move to a new burrow several times a year.

Burrows are used for sleeping, to

*After winter rains, spring flowers bloom around this kit fox burrow.*

*When making their dens, kit foxes (left) often enlarge the empty burrows of badgers (right) or other animals.*

escape predators, for protection from the weather, and as safe places to raise pups. A typical kit fox burrow is about 14 feet (4.3 meters) long and about 3 feet (.91 meter) deep. It has a narrow tunnel that widens at the deepest part to form a small cavity or room. A new den may have only one entrance, but more entrances are usually added and more tunnels dug as the den continues to be used over several years. In large burrows, some tunnels may be used as bathrooms or as storage rooms for food or trash. A mound of bare dirt usually surrounds the entrance to a den. The kit fox may also dig a small hole under a rock or bush near the entrance to its burrow and rest there during the day. Separate burrows, some distance away from the dens of other kit foxes, are used for raising pups.

## FAMILY LIFE

Foxes are able to mate for the first time when they are nine to ten months old, although in some cases females do not mate and have pups until they are nearly two.

For most North American foxes, the mating season is in the winter. At that time a male, or *dog fox,* and a female, or *vixen,* form a pair. For several weeks they hunt and rest together, and the female explores various den sites as possible places to have her pups. Usually, foxes form single pairs for mating, but with kit foxes a male will occasionally mate with more than one female. Then the females and their pups share one large burrow or live in burrows that are close to one another.

One sign of a fox's readiness to mate is a strong skunklike odor in its urine. The smell is especially strong in the urine of the male. After a pair has mated, the female is pregnant for seven to eight weeks. While she is waiting to give birth, she moves into the burrow, cleans it out, and makes it ready for her pups. The male fox may share the burrow with her or live by himself in a den nearby.

*Young kit foxes snuggle with their mother.*

The number of pups in a fox litter varies from one to as many as fourteen, depending on the species. A mother kit fox usually has four or five pups in a litter. At birth, the tiny pups are about 6 inches (15.4 centimeters) long and weigh less than a quarter of a pound (.11 kilogram). They are covered with short, dark, woolly fur.

A mother kit fox stays with her pups constantly during their first few weeks of life. She curls around them to keep them warm and licks their fur to keep them clean. When the pups get hungry, they nuzzle their mother's belly and drink milk from her teats.

Newborn fox pups are helpless, and their eyes are shut tight. The eyes open ten to twelve days later and are a gray-blue color. By the time the foxes are adults, their eye color has changed to yellowish brown.

While the female kit fox cares for her new pups in the den, the male fox goes hunting and brings back food for her to eat. When the pups are about two weeks old, the female leaves them for the first time and goes hunting too. She returns to the den regularly so that the pups can nurse.

The pups grow quickly inside the den. When they are about two weeks old, their first teeth come in. About a week later, they begin to suck and chew at the pieces of meat their parents have brought back to the den. Milk continues to be the pups' main food until they are about five weeks old. When they reach that age their mother begins to feed them less often, and they gradually switch to a diet of meat.

*Two kit fox pups explore.*

As the fox pups grow, they become bigger and stronger. When they are approximately a month old, they scramble out of the den for the first time. Each month-old pup weighs about a pound (.45 kilogram), and its short newborn coat is covered with soft light-colored fur.

Under their mother's watchful eye, the young foxes explore near the entrance to the den. They jump and pounce on one another, chase insects, and dig in the loose dirt. These playful activities help make their muscles strong and develop their coordination. Although their parents continue to provide food for them until they are six months old or more, the pups must soon learn to hunt for themselves.

The pups practice their hunting skills by scavenging fruits and catching insects near the den. When they are three to four months old, they are ready to go on their first hunting trip with their parents. At first the frisky pups are clumsy and make so much noise that they scare away their prey. Gradually they learn how to stalk an animal slowly and quietly so that it can be captured by surprise.

*A mother kit fox (left) watches over her playful pups (above and below).*

*A kit fox descends from a rocky ledge.*

By the time the kit fox pups are seven to eight months old, they have learned how to hunt and take care of themselves. Kit fox pups stay with their parents somewhat longer than the pups of other fox species, but by fall it is time for them to go off on their own. Usually, kit fox pups leave the area where they were born and find new places to live. This way, they will not have to compete with their parents for food.

Sometimes one or more of the young kit foxes stay with their parents. They may share a large den or occupy another den nearby. A young adult female will sometimes assist her parents in rearing the next litter of pups instead of mating and having her own. This kind of helping behavior occurs with other fox species as well. A fox that helps her parents increases the chances that the new pups will be strong and healthy. She also gains valuable experience that will aid her in bringing up her own litter in the future.

In most fox species, the male and female separate after their pups are grown. In the next breeding season they may become a pair again, or they may find new mates. With kit foxes, however, pairs often stay together for their whole lives.

*Kit foxes (left and above).*

## FOX TALK

Like other canids, foxes use a variety of sounds to communicate. They bark or growl as warnings to one another or to predators that come too close. If a fox is trapped or cornered, it makes croaking noises. When pups and their parents become separated, they make high-pitched calls to let one another know where they are.

Foxes also communicate with body language. A fox holds its tail up and lays its ears back to signal that it is ready to attack. A submissive fox crouches and holds its tail between its legs or along its side. When the tail is held in an upside-down U shape, it means the fox is in a playful mood.

Foxes have a good sense of smell and can identify one another by odor. Like other canids, a fox has a scent gland underneath its tail that produces a strong musky odor. When two foxes meet, they sniff each other's tails. As foxes move about, they also leave scented "calling cards" in their urine and feces to let other foxes know that they have been in the area. Some fox species do this to mark their territories—the smell tells other foxes to keep out. Kit foxes are not as territorial as other kinds of foxes and often have hunting territories that overlap.

*Predators of kit fox pups include bobcats (above) and golden eagles (right).*

## DANGERS IN THE WILD

Because of their size and quickness, adult foxes are rarely caught and eaten by other animals. Young pups, on the other hand, must watch out for predators, such as hawks, eagles, and coyotes. Bobcats and badgers, which are small enough to get into a kit fox den, can also threaten young pups.

The biggest dangers to kit foxes, as with other foxes, come from humans. Some foxes are killed by cars as they cross highways at night, and others are killed by hunters. Many kit foxes die when they eat poisoned bait that ranchers put out to kill coyotes. In a few states where kit foxes are well established in the wild, people are allowed to trap them for their fur. When they are kept in captivity, kit foxes can live as long as twenty years. In the wild, though, where they must contend with the weather, uncertain food supplies, competition with other foxes, and the danger of natural predators, they rarely live more than seven years.

## PEOPLE AND FOXES

Foxes have always had a close association with humans and often inhabit areas near people. Their ability to evade predators and their nighttime activities have helped earn them a reputation for crafty or sly behavior. Foxes often play tricky or clever roles in stories or songs. In some places they have been revered as deities or feared as evil spirits. Some people dislike foxes because they do occasionally prey on chickens or eat the eggs of game birds. Much more often, they benefit people by keeping rats, mice, and other pests under control. As with other predators, foxes are an important part of the balance of nature.

Foxes are fascinating animals whose adaptable natures, cunning, and quickness have enabled them to live in a wide variety of habitats. The tiny kit fox, with its large ears, small size, and quick reflexes, is a good example of how one fox species has adapted to special conditions—the desert and dry plains. As with other foxes, kit foxes are difficult to observe in the wild, so for most people the best way to become familiar with their behavior is by watching them in a zoo or animal park.

As we learn more about all species of foxes, we will better understand what they need in order to live, and we can better appreciate how these bushy-tailed relatives of the dog are among the most successful of all predators.

# INDEX

Photographs are in **boldface.**